MASS OF THE CHILI

1. Kyrie

*Words by Thomas Ken (1637–1711)

Printed in Great Britain

OXFORD UNIVERSITY PRESS, MUSIC DEPARTMENT, GREAT CLARENDON STREET, OXFORD OX2 6DP

4

sa - cri - fice._____ Re - deem thy mis - spent time that's past, Live this

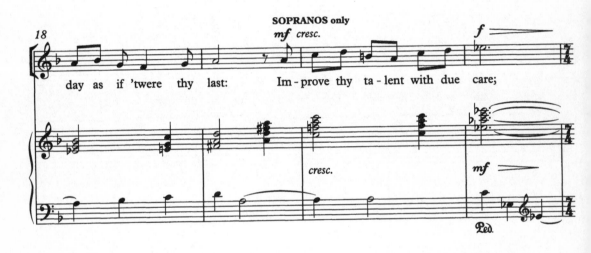

day as if 'twere thy last: Im - prove thy ta - lent with due care;

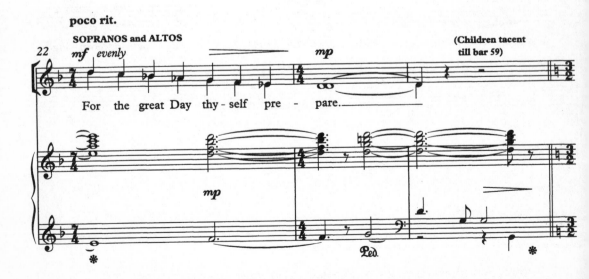

For the great Day thy - self pre - pare._____

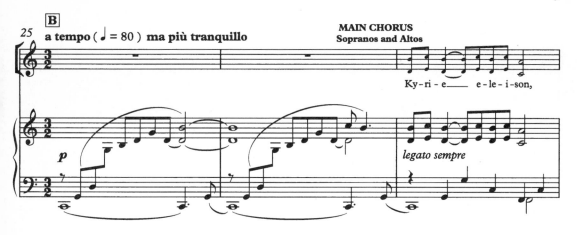

6

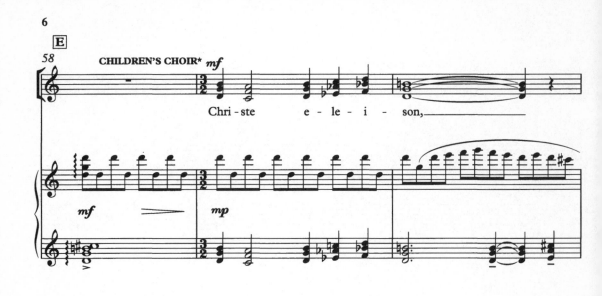

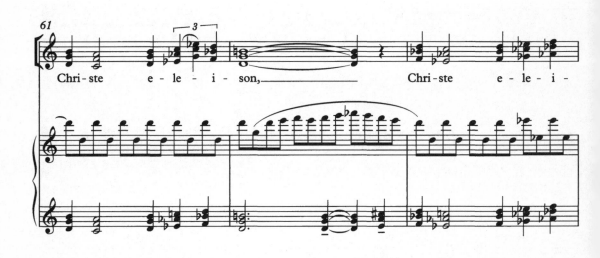

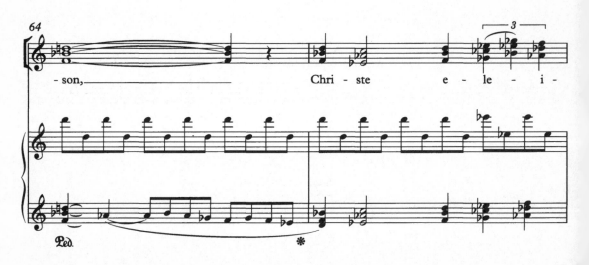

*In bars 59–66, the lowest voice is optional, but in bars 67–70 the voices should divide into three as shown.

8

2. Gloria

10

*It is suggested that both the 1st and 2nd voices should consist of a mixture of sopranos and altos.

12

13

14

3. Sanctus and Benedictus

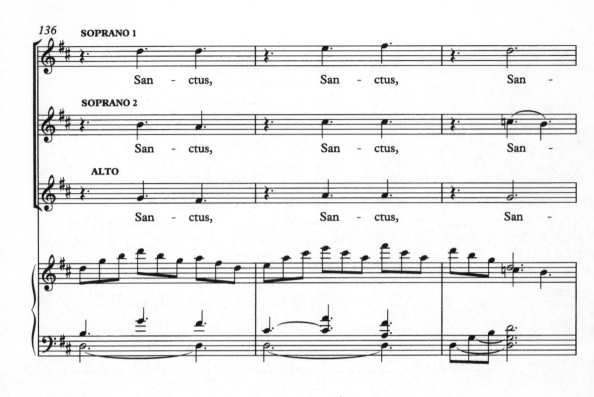

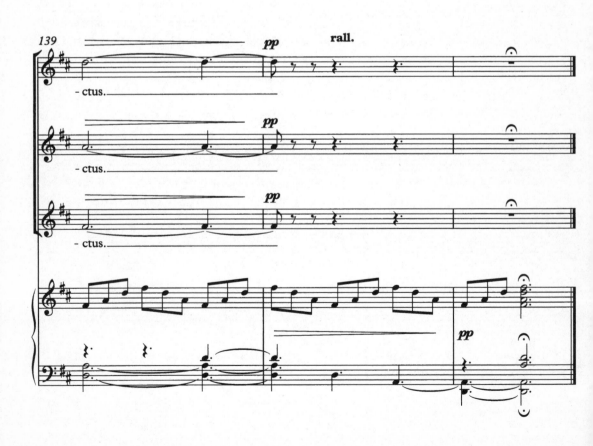

4. Agnus Dei

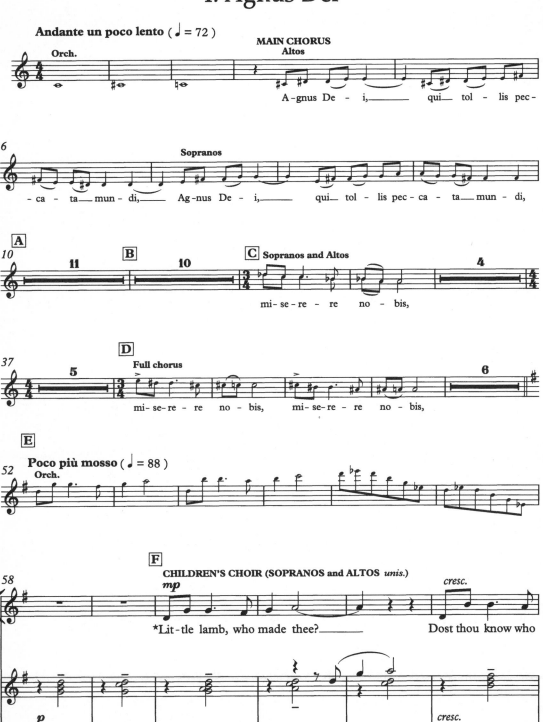

* Text by William Blake (1757–1827)

5. Finale (Dona nobis pacem)

24

25

*Text by Thomas Ken (1637–1711)
†If preferred, the alto part in the children's choir from here to the end may be sung an octave higher.

104

wings.

- cem. _____ do-na no - bis pa - cem,

_mp_ _dim._ _p_

109

CHILDREN'S CHOIR
SOPRANO 1

K

f ma dolce

Praise God, from whom all bless - ings

SOPRANO 2

f ma dolce

Praise God, from

ALTO

Altos   Sopranos

do - na, do - na no - bis, do - na

mp tranquillo